T0198975

Rescuing Molly

Daryl Michel

This book is a work of non-fiction. Unless otherwise noted, the author and the publisher make no explicit guarantees as to the accuracy of the information contained in this book and in some cases, names of people and places have been altered to protect their privacy.

WestBow Press books may be ordered through booksellers or by contacting:

WestBow Press
A Division of Thomas Nelson & Zondervan
1663 Liberty Drive
Bloomington, IN 47403
www.westbowpress.com
1 (866) 928-1240

Because of the dynamic nature of the Internet, any web addresses or links contained in this book may have changed since publication and may no longer be valid. The views expressed in this work are solely those of the author and do not necessarily reflect the views of the publisher, and the publisher hereby disclaims any responsibility for them.

Any people depicted in stock imagery provided by Getty Images are models, and such images are being used for illustrative purposes only.
Certain stock imagery © Getty Images.

ISBN: 978-1-9736-7335-4 (sc)
ISBN: 978-1-9736-7336-1 (e)

Library of Congress Control Number: 2019912764

Print information available on the last page.

WestBow Press rev. date: 09/12/2019

WESTBOW
PRESS®
A DIVISION OF THOMAS NELSON
& ZONDERVAN

Hello there friends! I am Molly a 10 year old Bishon Frese dog who used to live with my mom Pam. Mom Pam and I lived on a canopy lined street with oak trees.

We had a screened in porch where I had my area to do my business. My area was covered by yellow stones with a pretty bright flowered bush. Mom Pam always kept it clean after I did my business. There were times we did not go for a walk.

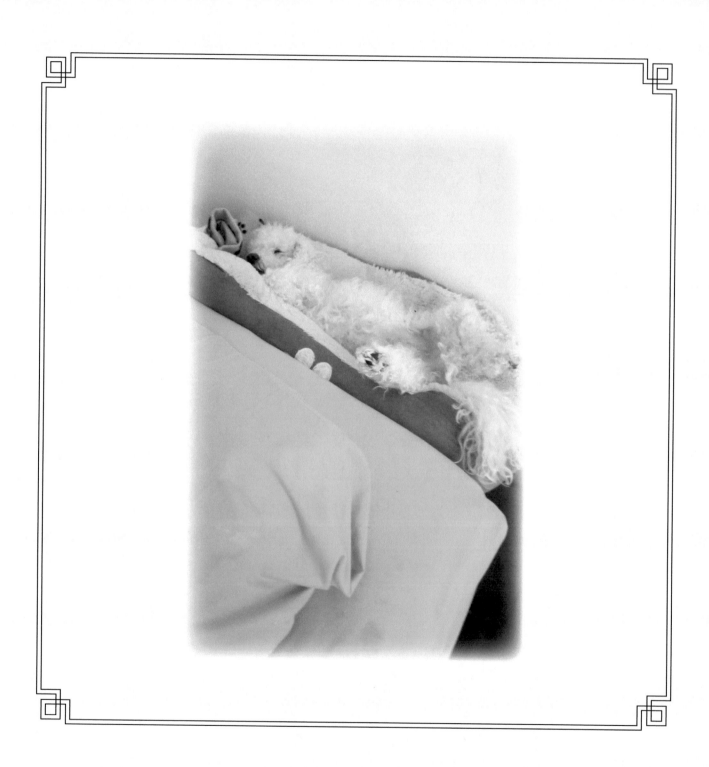

Recently my Mom Pam went to heaven and now lives on a white puffy cloud. We did almost everything together. We went on walks, spent lots of time together in our house after walks. most of the time we were in the kitchen or our bedroom. We made a good team.

Sometimes we would go for long rides to a groomer, she made me look beautiful! I was happy when the grooming was done.

The car ride home was fun since I got to sit and look out the window. I could admire how pretty I looked.

Later we started going to a groomer very close to home. Mom Pam was never very happy with my cut. We found 'Hollywood Diva' which Mom felt was more my style and hers.

Mom Pam was my only friend. I was the only company in the house for her since no one came over. Mom Pam was old and lonely so I tried to make her smile and keep her spirits up.

Sometimes Mom went to the theater, shopping or many restaurants. She liked eating out. Restaurants were her favorite places since they were shared with friends. I would hear her talk to friends on the phone.

Sherry was one of her favorite people, I could tell. She smiled when she was talking to her.

One night Mom Pam went to sleep and did not wake up. I felt alone, scared, hungry and thirsty. I had drunk all the water in my bowl. The one thing I could do now was bark very loud so someone could hear me. I barked louder and louder.... but no one came at first.

I needed help so I went by the front door.

Three policemen came into the house within a few days checking on us. I was surprised but grateful since my tummy was hungry. I figured they would find my food and put it in my bowl.

Then I was wondering if I could be taken for a walk since I wanted to go outside. Neighbors came with yummy treats and more food. Even though I am shy, I jumped at having more food. Loved the treats.

One neighbor Alexa was comforting and took me for a walk. Really needed to stretch my legs! Alexa gave a lot of hugs.

Afterwards a lady with a uniform took my leash and put me into a large cold van. It was scary and I was alone.

We rode for what seemed to be a long time. Finally we arrived at a big building. OH NO this is not a house! Many dogs were barking. It definitely was not a house! I was put into a large crate.

They gave me a small blanket so I cried myself to sleep while shaking.

Alexa came with a friend two days later and rescued me Molly from the big building!

I proudly walked out of the big building on a nice new leash. We got into a comfy silver car in which Alexa held me close hugging me tightly.

We slowly drove to a pretty blue house with big windows and lots of flowers. I was sad since this was not my house.

It was then I realized Mom Pam was gone forever. I was not going back to my house with Mom Pam.

It took many weeks before I felt at home with my new family. I had belly aches, sadness and missed my Mom Pam.

Alexa took good care of me so slowly I started feeling safe. Alexa had a sister named Zoe who loved giving hugs and walking me.

This family had 2 dogs already Lexi and Connor. Lexi seemed to be the one in charge. I was not used to other dogs. This definitely took time to get used to but this was my new family. I was happy they rescued me.

Also I now have a father named Stuart at my new home. never had one of those. Stuart has a wife named Michele who give lots of hugs too! We go on very long walks.

I love my new family and now I smile every day.

Printed in the United States
By Bookmasters